Which Way Did They Go?

As you read this book, look for characters from these stories: *Three Little Kittens, The Frog Prince, The Tortoise and the Hare,* and *Little Red Riding Hood.*

"Did you see three little kittens?"
asked Mama Cat.

"Which way did they go?"

"Did you see a turtle?" asked the rabbit.

“Which way did he go?”

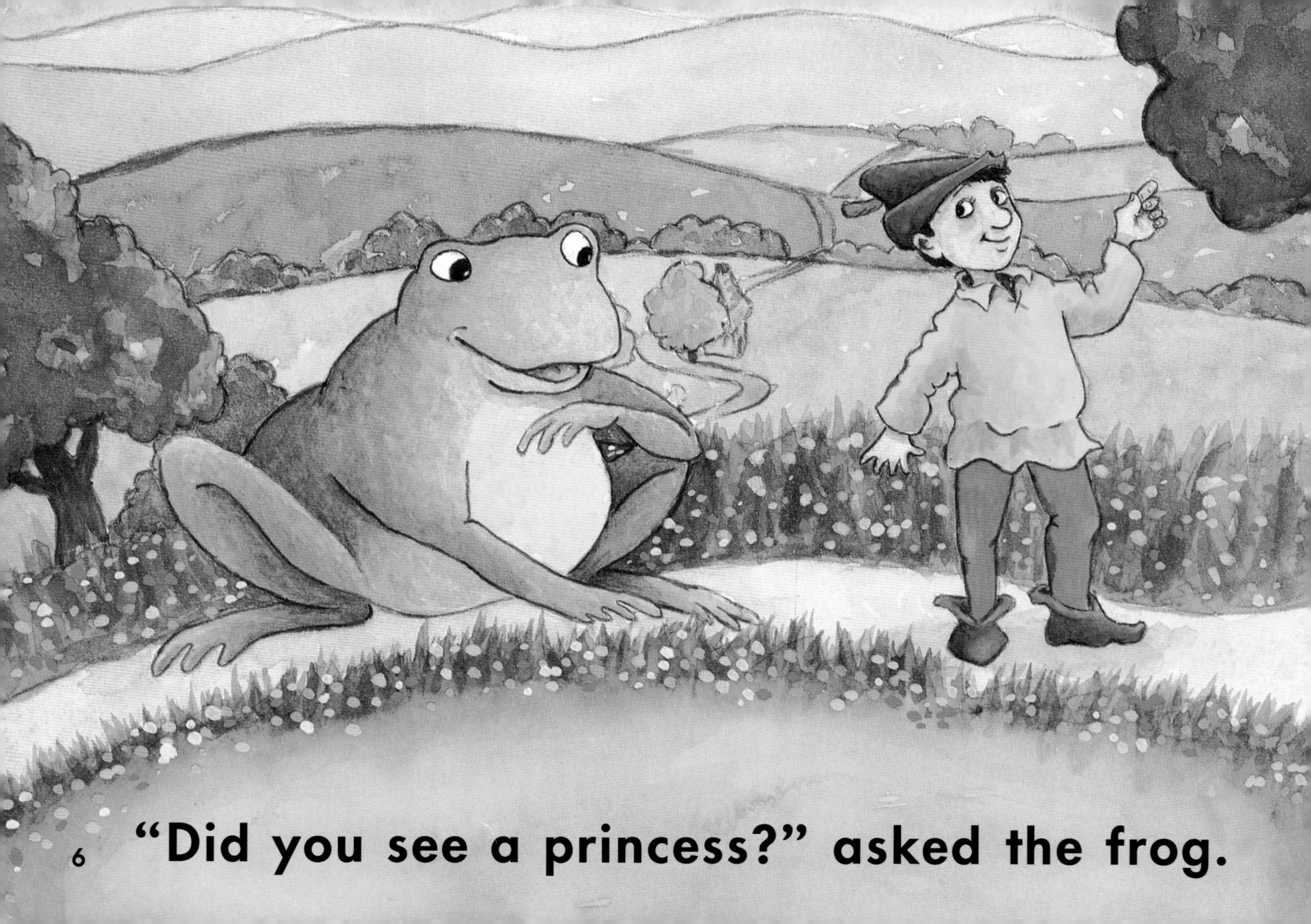

“Did you see a princess?” asked the frog.

“Which way did she go?”

"Did you see a little girl?" asked the wolf.
"Which way did she go?"

"I will go *this* way," said the wolf.

The three little kittens went that way.
Mama Cat went that way.

The turtle and the rabbit went that way.

The princess and the frog went that way.

The little girl went that way.
Where did they all go?

This is where they all went.

But where did the wolf go?

This is where the wolf went!